# SUMMARY

# Start With Why

### Book by Simon Sinek

*How Great Leaders Inspire Everyone to Take Action*

**Instant-Summary**

# © Copyright 2017 - Present.
# All rights reserved.

This document is geared towards providing reliable information in regards to the topic and issue covered. The publication is sold with the idea that the publisher is not required to render accounting, officially permitted, or otherwise, qualified services. If advice is necessary, legal or professional, a practiced individual in the profession shall be ordered.

- From a Declaration of Principles which was accepted and approved equally by a Committee of the American Bar Association and a Committee of Publishers and Associations.

In no way is it legal to reproduce, duplicate, or transmit any part of this document in either electronic means or in printed format. Recording of this publication is strictly prohibited and any storage of this document is not allowed unless with written permission from the publisher. All rights reserved.

The information provided herein is stated to be truthful and consistent, in that any liability, in terms of inattention or otherwise, by any usage or abuse of any policies, processes, or directions contained within is solely and completely the responsibility of the recipient reader. Under no circumstances will any legal responsibility or blame be held against the publisher for any reparation, damages, or monetary loss due to the information herein, either directly or indirectly.

Respective authors own all copyrights not held by the publisher.

## *Before we proceed ...*

Feel free to follow us on social media to get notified of future summaries.

1. Facebook: BookSummaries
   https://www.facebook.com/BookSummaries-1060732983986564/

2. Instagram: BookSummaries
   https://www.instagram.com/booksummaries/

# TABLE OF CONTENTS

INTRODUCTION ............................................................. 5

SUMMARY ...................................................................... 6

    PART 1: WHY SHOULD WE ASK WHY? ...................... 6

    PART 2: MANIPULATION VERSUS INSPIRATION: WHY SOME PEOPLE TEND TO MANIPULATE ............ 8

    PART 3: IT IS MORE THAN JUST AN OPINION ........ 11

    PART 4: CLARITY, DISCIPLINE AND CONSISTENCY AS KEY FACTORS FOR SUCCESS ...... 12

    PART 5: THE IMPORTANCE OF TRUST ..................... 13

    PART 6: STARTING WITH 'WHY' AND CONTINUING WITH 'HOW' ......................................... 16

ANALYSIS ...................................................................... 18

QUIZ .............................................................................. 20

QUIZ ANSWERS ............................................................ 23

CONCLUSION ............................................................... 24

# INTRODUCTION

*Start with Why* is a book written by Simon Sinek. Someone may ask, *what is so special about this book?* In this book, Sinek discusses success, but not in the usual, "follow these steps to achieve anything you want," way. Sinek uses a different approach than readers tend to find in other literature of the same type.

The very first premise that the author uses to lead us into his book is a premise that contains one simple word: why. Why do some people reach success while others do not? Why do some groups manage to team-up and endure challenges, thus succeeding, while others fail to do so? What is it that makes some people different from others when it comes to achieving success? The entire book revolves around that question word. But the interesting thing about it, which eventually leads to even more interesting conclusion, is that there is an answer to this "why." Sinek uses many examples from real life and from people he knew or had researched, and shows how they managed to succeed. By using these examples, the author shows his readers that if others can succeed, so can we. When it comes to practical answers to "why," the author invests significant effort in finding all the answers.

*Start with Why* is an intriguing and fascinating read, which will surely make readers ask themselves this simple, yet tricky question: why?

# SUMMARY

## PART 1:
## WHY SHOULD WE ASK WHY?

The first part of the book opens with this simple question, which will be used throughout the entire book: why? Why some people, like Martin Luther King, Jr., succeeded in doing the things they did, while others could not achieve the same "amount" of success? Martin Luther King had many experiences, which he shared with many people. But the interesting thing is that his experiences were not always unique and "one of a kind." Despite that, King managed to lead people and people listened to and believed what he was saying. Another example is Apple Computers. Even though Apple is not the leading manufacturer of personal computers, the company somehow manages to lead in the entire computer industry.

The question is, *why does this happen?* Why did King manage to do what he did and why is Apple so successful?

The first answer given by the author is *inspiration*.

People and organizations can inspire others, and thus lead them to bigger success. People within one organization can lead other people and influence their way of thinking and working by inspiring them. This is actually one of the biggest secrets of why some leaders succeed in what they do and some do not. This is also why many leaders aim to reach out to others. The easiest and the best way to reach out to others is to inspire them.

What happens inside a company when someone inspires others?

The first thing that happens "inside" the people is that they get this "surge" of energy and motivation. People want to do more, want to stay longer at work, and want to go the "extra mile," not because they have to, but because they want to. When someone is inspired, that person will give "110%" in everything they do.

When a person is inspired and motivated, that person is also ready to endure personal suffering and pain, even potential damage that can be done to that person. An inspired person will be motivated, will have stronger will, and be more optimistic, especially when it comes to challenges. Also, when people are inspired, they become loyal. Loyalty is very important and to have loyal customers, clients, co-workers and employees means long-lasting success – not just survival, but development, for the entire company.

# PART 2: MANIPULATION VERSUS INSPIRATION: WHY SOME PEOPLE TEND TO MANIPULATE

In this part of the book, the author says that there are only two ways of influencing human behavior: inspiring it and manipulating it. Sadly, many people prefer manipulation over inspiration and use manipulation when it comes to influencing the opinions and actions of others.

Why does manipulation happen in the first place?

Let's look at companies. When a company does not have a clear goal or when a company does not know what the needs of their potential customers are, they manipulate. One typical manipulation is when a company drops the price on the products or services they offer. We see this example on an everyday basis.

Manipulation often works and has its benefits. For example, by dropping the prices of products, businesses manipulate customers into buying the products more than they used to. But there is one big flaw of manipulation. When manipulating someone, the main goal is to get something from that person. But even after successfully manipulating someone, whoever is being manipulated will never be loyal. So the price of manipulation is loyalty, which is exactly what every truly successful company seeks.

Also with manipulation, people will never stick to whoever manipulates them. There is another big difference between manipulation and inspiration. Inspiration "inspires" people and motivates them to stick together in both good and bad times. On the contrary, manipulation will never motivate people to stick together when bad times come. Manipulation is also carried out by any means necessary, including fear, and this is another reason why people usually run away when the bad times comes.

Motivated and inspired people believe in one truth and that truth tells them that whatever they do, they are in this together, united. This is another reason why inspiration should definitely be a must and why manipulation should be entirely removed.

But how do leaders inspire their employees and their associates?

Here the author explains something that he likes to call "The Golden Circle." The Gold Circle consists of three smaller circles, "Why," "How," and "What."

Let's begin with "What" first.

"What" suggests that every single organization and firm on the planet knows *what* they are supposed to do. This means that the organization can easily describe the products or articles they are producing and selling.

"How" means that, within the company, the employees know *how* to do the things they do. They know how to produce a particular article and how to sell it.

"Why" is something that very few people actually know. This means that very few people know *why* the company they are working for is as successful as it is.

When it comes to earning money, the author says that money is a result of working and that earning money does not consider the "why" part of the circle. "Why" comes from a person's beliefs, purpose and reasons for doing something.

What happens when people communicate with the outside?

When people communicate with the outside they often say "what," and sometimes "how," but almost never "why." There is a big difference between "why" and "what." Most people buy things because of what the product is. For example, people buy smartphones because they are nice, simple to use and have many Apps pre-installed. But *why* should someone really buy a smartphone? The answer on that is that a smartphone is not only nice, easy to use and loaded with Apps, but it also makes communication much easier and can be used as a small computer, thus making the entire life of the user much easier overall.

# PART 3: IT IS MORE THAN JUST AN OPINION

In this part of the book, Sinek speaks about how people love being around other people and organizations who share similar beliefs and opinions. That is precisely why many leaders aim to connect their clients with their products.

For example, when producing technology gadgets, leaders of those companies always aim towards their potential users. They are trying to connect with them and they are trying to show them that this particular company "thinks" the way they think and thus has developed this particular gadget. This is connected to a leader's ability to make us feel as if we belong. When a leader succeeds in making us feel as if we belong somewhere, we will also feel greatly inspired by that leader. Leaders who can do this lead their companies in a radically different way than the leaders of other companies. These leaders go with "Why" first, not "What," because they know that their buyers and users of their products and services want to know *why* they should buy exactly that smartphone.

This is the main difference between good and the best leaders. The best leaders know *why* we need something that we need, even before we know that we need it. They are winning our attention, our loyalty and our hearts. That is why great leaders know how to properly use "Why" in whatever they do. By saying "Why" first, companies spread a message that they know who they are, what their goal is, and why their goal is precisely what it is.

# PART 4: CLARITY, DISCIPLINE AND CONSISTENCY AS KEY FACTORS FOR SUCCESS

If a leader wants The Golden Circle to work to its fullest potential, they must learn how to use "Why," "How," and "What" properly.

The first thing they need to understand is the clarity of "Why." Before doing something, a person, a company or a leader must know why they do what they do.

Second is the discipline of "How." The discipline of "How" tells us how exactly we will do something that we do or something that we plan to do. When we understand how something is going to work, we will have significantly more influence in everything we do. When we find out how to do something, we need to find someone who will share our goals and we need to maintain discipline, which will eventually lead us toward achieving our goal.

The third this is the consistency of "What."

"Why" is someone's belief that something will succeed. "How" reflects on every action that the person takes towards realization of that belief. "What" is our actions. Our services, products, PR – everything that we have done while trying to achieve a particular goal – goes under "What." But all those things must be consistent. With consistency people will see that we are certain about the things we do, and that we are confident in what we do, how we do it, and why we do it.

# PART 5:
# THE IMPORTANCE OF TRUST

This chapter is dedicated to trust. The author says that when "Why, What, and How" are in balance, then trust is built and that value is visible and appreciated.

Being a leader is different from leading. When someone is a leader, that means the person has the highest rank. But when someone leads, that means something else. A person who leads, leads people not because of some external, higher goals, such as better payment or because someone has to follow that particular someone. This person leads because people trust them. People trust this person's judgment and they trust that this person will do the best they possibly can for the good of those who follow.

But to find people who will believe what you believe and who will thus follow you almost unconditionally is not an easy task. To find these people, recruitment is needed. It is necessary to find people who share the same interest as the person who will then lead them towards reaching their mutual goal. Here is also an important "Why." Because of this "Why," people will follow someone. That is why companies that are the most successful employ people who are already motivated and skilled, so all they need to do is to inspire them. When they are inspired, these employees will not work for the company. They will actually work for themselves. An inspired person does not think in terms of "I have to do this so that my company becomes even more successful and so that my boss compliments my work." Instead this person thinks, "I am working like this because my company inspires me to do my best."

By having a strong sense of "Why," people become a lot more productive and loyal because it changes their entire perception of the work they do. This is the main reason why companies should develop a strong sense of "Why."

What are the most important "duties," which every good leader needs to have?

Most people think that being a good leader means bringing all the best ideas and innovations, but the truth is a bit different. A good leader does not need to invent new ideas. What a good leader has to do is find and create an environment in which good ideas will have the opportunity to be born.

What about trust within the organization?

The most distinctive fact which distinguishes good organizations from great ones, is that in great organizations people feel protected.

A feeling of protection is created when employees within the organization know that in case of trouble or need their boss, their superiors, and their colleagues will look out for them. Also, if employees within the organization are treated fairly and right, they will treat the outside world right. This means that if a salesperson is treated right by their superiors, they will also treat their potential customers and clients right. By doing that, they create more chances for potential clients and customers to become real clients and customers. And by offering them the right service and by treating them right, they will give those customers the opportunity to see that the company, which that salesman represents, is honest and treats everyone right. Thus they will want to use that company's services more when the need comes.

But is it possible to rally those who believe? We will find out about that in the next chapter.

# PART 6:
# STARTING WITH 'WHY' AND CONTINUING WITH 'HOW'

In this chapter, the author speaks about the perfect combination of people who know how to use "Why" with those who know how to use "How" in the best way. When these two groups join together, success is at hand.

The reason for that is because the "Why" type of people are actually visionaries. These people have a vision, a picture of why something would be the way it is supposed to be. But they often do not know how to properly apply that vision and how to make it work. That is why they need "How" type of people, because "How" people live in the present moment. "How" people are realists and they know how things work in the present moment. When "Why" visionaries and "How" realists join together, vision very quickly becomes reality and success is imminent.

But even though there are people who understand how things work and why a leader's vision is the way it is, for true success more is needed. A leader needs to know how to spread their vision in order to reach as many people as possible. Without the message, there will simply not be enough people who will get the leader's idea. Then there is a big risk that idea the idea will be aborted before it can produce results. This is a perfect situation for the best use of the Golden Circle. With the proper use of it and with the successful use of "Why," "What," and "How," leader(s) can properly spread their ideas to the outside, with the help of people who know how to do this and what resources to use to achieve the desired result.

But what happens when "Why" becomes unclear?

In that case, problems will arise. If "Why" is not clear on the inside, it will also be unclear on the outside. Even though people can still show some achievements and they may still "chase" success, achievement and success are two different things. Achievement is gained when someone pursues and gets "What" that person wanted. Success, on the other hand, is achieved when a person gets the answer to "Why" that person did what they did in the first place.

There is also another risk.

When a company is small, the question of "Why" is easier to follow and the leader will have fewer problems with it. But the real problem arrives when a company becomes larger. With a larger company (or organization) the "Why" can, and often does, become unclear. In this case, the message that the leader sends to the outside can become diluted. That is why focus on the original and primary "Why" is crucial. With that in mind, the company will always stay close to its primary goals for "why we do what we do" and the message that will be spread will reach the required amount of people for "Why" to reach its maximum potential.

The summary ends here.

# ANALYSIS

When starting a business, people often make many mistakes and are not even aware of it. When thinking about their ideas, and the products and services that their company needs to provide, people often find themselves on a "different track" from the people who will be using their products or services. This book is trying to decipher this puzzle, in which three main questions arise: "Why," "How," and "What."

Personally I think that the book is a bit too simple. Someone may ask: *How is it possible for a book that deals with such important questions to possibly be too simple?* That is a great question. The answer to this is that the author manages to answer the three questions of "Why," "How," and "What," and not just that. He manages to fully describe the entire use for "Why, How, and What." By fully understanding how these three questions, when joined together, function to bring success, a reader can have a complete vision for how a single company or even a complex organizational system should work. And the right word is "should," because, as we know and as the author suggests, many companies and organizations either do not know how to properly use these three questions, or use them in a wrong way. The book's title *Start with Why* is actually just right, because Sinek uses this simple question word to provide answers to many questions, which are not simple to answer.

As we read the book we actually go through the entire complex system of how, a company works and how it should work, how an idea is implemented in most companies and how it should be implemented. We read why the question "Why" is truly the most important question and why should we always start with it and how the other two questions also work towards accomplishing the goal.

And the goal is divided into several sub-sections: successful discovery of the leader's vision (Why), successful implementation of that vision with the help of the people who are right for the job by determining how everything will work (How), and determining what the main activity of the company will be (What). To be able to successfully combine and implement these three questions other requirements must be met, such as finding the best way to reach the outside and the people who will get the idea and the leader's vision. To do that a leader should surround himself with the proper people. This means that he should implement his ideas with the help of people who share his dreams and visions.

Overall, *Start with Why* is a book with many answers, which are provided through answering only three questions. By reading the book, readers will not only get a better understanding of how something works, but they will also understand why vision, ideas, and "Why" are the most important ingredients in building success.

# QUIZ

This quiz is written for readers who liked the book and want to either learn something new or test their knowledge. Questions are easy to answer and their answers can be found either in the 'summary' or in the 'quiz answers' sections.

Let's get started then.

## QUESTION 1

What is the most important question that each leader should ask himself when trying to spread his message to the people?

a) 'How' to do that?

b) 'Why' to do that?

c) 'What' do I want to say with my message?

d) None of the above.

## QUESTION 2

Why is inspiration so important when it comes to working with people?

a) Inspiration makes people to do things voluntarily.

b) When inspired, people will feel connected and will work for themselves and not feel the pressure that something 'has to be done'.

c) Inspiration invokes new ideas in people.

d) Everything above.

e) 'a' and 'c'.

## QUESTION 3

Who are actually people who always start with the question 'Why'?

    a) They are evolutionists.

    b) They are revolutionists.

    c) They are visionaries.

    d) They are people who are working hard towards achieving their goals.

## QUESTION 4

"A feeling of protection is created when employees within the organization know that in case of trouble and/or need their boss, their superiors, their colleagues will look out for them."

        FALSE        TRUE

## QUESTION 5

What will happen within a company if 'Why' becomes unclear on the inside?

    a) If 'Why' becomes clear on the inside it will be a lot harder to make it clear on the outside.

    b) The message will not be spread to the people.

c) 'a' and 'b'.

d) If 'Why' becomes unclear on the inside it will also become unclear on the outside.

## QUESTION 6

There is a name for 'Why, What' and 'How' joined together. The author calls it...

a) ...the Golden Square.

b) ...the Golden Triangle.

c) ...the Silver Circle.

d) ...the Golden Circle.

## QUESTION 7

Why some companies tend to manipulate their customers and clients?

a) They manipulate because they need to earn a lot of money fast.

b) They manipulate because they do not really know the needs of their customers.

c) They manipulate because their 'higher-ups' told them to do so.

d) Everything above.

# QUIZ ANSWERS

QUESTION 1 – a

QUESTION 2 – d

QUESTION 3 – c

QUESTION 4 – TRUE

QUESTION 5 – d

QUESTION 6 – d

QUESTION 7 – b

# CONCLUSION

*Start with Why* is a book in which the author speaks about ideas, visions, trust, manipulation and inspiration. All this is discussed by answering three simple questions: why, how and what.

It is sort of a surprise how Sinek manages to comprehend and to explain as much as possible of these topics by simply giving answers to how to properly use these three questions and then forming the so-called "Golden Circle," where "Why, How, and What," will perfectly interconnect and fulfill each other in a perfect pattern. This will then lead to success that is known to people like Martin Luther King, Jr. and Steve Jobs. I believe that readers can learn a lot from this book. Not just how everything works within one company or why some companies manipulate their customers and others do not, but something much more than that. I believe that after reading this book, readers will have a much clearer image about why an idea and vision is actually a vital segment of success and why we should follow our "Why" in the first place.

Another thing that the author tries to teach his readers is that it is not about competition with others. It is about competing with ourselves. When we compete with ourselves and when we get a clear image of why we do what we do and how to do it, others will also want to help us, especially if they share the same interests as we do.

I recommend reading (and if possible buying) *Start with Why*. Not only is it an interesting and educational read, but it also presents this whole idea of competition and working towards accomplishing the goal in entirely new and unique way.

*Start with Why* definitely deserves a "thumb up."

# Thank You, and more...

Thank you for spending your time to read this book, I hope now you hold a greater knowledge about **Start with Why.**

There are like-minded individuals like you who would like to learn about **Start with Why,** this information can be useful for them as well. So, I would highly appreciate if you post a good review on amazon kindle where you purchased this book. And to share it in your social media (Facebook, Instagram, etc.)

Not only does it help me make a living, but it helps others obtain this knowledge as well. So I would highly appreciate it!!

www.amazon.com

# FURTHER READINGS

If you are interested in other book summaries, feel free to check out the summaries below.

    1- Summary - All the Light We Cannot See
       by Instant-Summary

       https://www.amazon.com//dp/B07653T57B/

    2- Summary – The Obstacle is the Way
       by Instant-Summary

       https://www.amazon.com/dp/B075PFY8CP/

*For more books by Instant-Summary, visit:

https://www.amazon.com/s/ref=nb_sb_noss?url=search-alias=aps&field-keywords=instant-summary

Made in the USA
San Bernardino, CA
06 September 2018